COUNTER CONTROL
FOR
CHAMPIONSHIP WRESTLING

COUNTER CONTROL FOR CHAMPIONSHIP WRESTLING

Ray F. Carson

SOUTH BRUNSWICK AND NEW YORK:
A. S. BARNES AND COMPANY
LONDON: THOMAS YOSELOFF LTD

A. S. Barnes and Co., Inc.
Cranbury, New Jersey 08512

Thomas Yoseloff Ltd
108 New Bond Street
London W1Y OQX, England

Library of Congress Cataloging in Publication Data

Carson, Ray F.   1939-
    Counter control for championship wrestling.

    Bibliography: p.
    Includes index.
    1. Wrestling.   I. Title.
GV1195.C333   796.8'12   74-30723
ISBN 0-498-01633-1

PRINTED IN THE UNITED STATES OF AMERICA

This book is dedicated to three people who, perhaps more than any others, were destined to give direction to my life:

Mr. James Manning, Principal of Gower School, Hinsdale, Illinois— a fine teacher and a man who can inspire boys to do better than they can

Miss Yvonne Smith, Freshman at Hinsdale High School, Hinsdale, Illinois—an intelligent, talented, and beautiful person

Dr. Chet Castellaw, Pastor of The First Church of Religious Science, San Diego, California—A man with profound insight into the psychology of human behavior

CONTENTS

ACKNOWLEDGMENTS

Gratitude is expressed to Gabriel Jesus Ruz and Alex Verduzco, members of the United States International University wrestling team, San Diego, California, for posing for the photographs used in this text.

"Gab" Ruz was the 1968 California Interscholastic Federation (C.I.F.) wrestling champion from Costa Mesa High School. While attending Santa Ana Junior College, he was Mexican National Champion twice and represented Mexico in the 1968 Olympic Games. In 1972 he was second in the N.A.I.A. Nationals and again represented Mexico in the Olympic Games.

Alex Verduzco has won countless titles. To date he has placed first in forty-eight tournaments. Before enrolling at U.S.I.U., he wrestled for Hawthorne High School and then El Camino Junior College. In 1972 he was first in the Far Western Greco Roman Olympic trials, California State Greco Roman Champion, and Arizona State Freestyle Champion.

I would also like to acknowledge Gomer Jones's and Charles (Bud) Wilkinson's excellent book *Modern Defensive Football** as being a particularly helpful reference in the writing of this text.

In preparation of the text, a special thanks is extended to the photographer, Mr. C. Wesley Beeson of Oceanside, California.

*Gomer Jones and Charles (Bud) Wilkinson. *Modern Defensive Football*. Englewood Cliffs, New Jersey: Prentice-Hall, Inc., 1960.

Gabriel Jesus Ruz.

Alex Verduzco.

COUNTER CONTROL
FOR
CHAMPIONSHIP WRESTLING

1

COUNTER CONTROL

NATURE OF CONTROL AND COUNTER CONTROL

There are two distinct phases to wrestling—control and counter control. The control phase, as depicted below, is an inherent part of every aspect of wrestling.

Takedown = Gaining Control
Escape   = Loss of Control
Reversal = Exchange of Control
Ride   = Maintenance of Control
Near Fall = High Level of Control
Pin   = Ultimate Control

Control is gained when the opponent is taken down to the mat from a neutral position. It is maintained when in the position of advantage. It is terminated when the opponent escapes or reverses. It is ultimate when the opponent's shoulders are held to the mat resulting in a fall.

The significance of the control phase is well expressed by George Martin in the following passage: "It will help the . . . coach to ever keep in mind that in wrestling each contestant is striving to gain CONTROL and to keep CONTROL of the opponent; or, on occasion, to escape from the CONTROL of the opponent. Football and basketball coaches stress the importance of controlling the ball; in wrestling one must control the opponent to win."*

* George Martin. *The Mechanics of Wrestling*. College Printing and Typing Co., Inc., 453 W. Gilman St., Madison, Wis., 1961, p. 11.

The second phase of wrestling is counter control. Counter control is the application of any skill, technique, or maneuver designed to oppose the restraining or directing influence that is imposed or attempting to be imposed by an opponent.

SIGNIFICANCE OF COUNTER CONTROL

Counter control is perhaps the most important single factor in winning wrestling. In assessing its significance, logic suggests that being apt at countering an opponent's efforts at control constitutes winning. If a wrestler can't be controlled, he can't be beaten. When counters are effectively employed the opponent cannot score. It logically follows that if the opponent does not score, defeat cannot be realized.

Countering is basic to success. A sound defense is a key ingredient in winning. Unless an opponent's attempts to gain, maintain, and terminate control can be countered, very few matches are going to be won. Effective countering limits the number of attempts the opponent has at gaining, maintaining, and terminating control. Therefore, when two offensively equal men meet, the match ends in favor of the better counter control wrestler.

It should always be remembered that THERE IS NO WRESTLING MOVE THAT CANNOT BE COUNTERED. Any move can, in most cases, be countered in several ways. Any of these counters will generally nullify the effectiveness of an attack. From a mathematical standpoint, winning can be realized through counter counter tactics since A SUCCESSFUL COUNTER COUNTS JUST AS MUCH AS A SUCCESSFUL ATTACK.

14

2
BASIC THEORY

POSITIONS TO AVOID

Wrestling is a contest of physical chess encompassing a series of moves and countermoves. As in chess, there are logical counters to every move. In addition, there are counters to counters, and more counters to these counters. In fact, there are probably as many methods of countering any one particular move as there are variations to that move.

Wrestling amounts to a multisuccession of moves, each of which begins with an attempt to gain, maintain, or terminate control, followed by a series of counters and re-counters.

The attacker initiates the series. He employs the initial move. This attacking move must, obviously, be executed from either a standing position or a position down on the mat. If executed from down on the mat, it must be performed in one or more of the following five positions:

1. the back
2. the stomach
3. the side
4. the buttocks
5. one or both knees.

Any move attempted from down on the mat has an equal if not greater chance of losing points by being countered than one attempted from standing. Those attempted from a standing position are the hardest to stop. They leave the wrestler in the safest position if countered.

It is hardest to score points against an opponent who initiates moves from standing. Any move made several feet above the mat will rarely score points for the wrestler countering it. However, countering the same move attempted within inches of the mat will generally result in points being scored.

TECHNIQUE SELECTION

Every move in wrestling possesses a degree of risk in being countered. Obviously, some moves are more easily countered than others. Their frequent ineffectiveness increases the likelihood of countering tactics gaining points.

The counter control wrestler is most likely to score when the opponent selects a technique that requires assuming one or more of the five positions to avoid.

The rules of the sport are established so that the closer the opponent's shoulder or scapula area is to the mat, the greater are the number of points that can be scored against him. The most desirable position to catch an opponent is on his back, since this is where the greatest potential exists for gaining points or a pin.

3
FUNDAMENTALS

CRITICISM

The emphasis in wrestling is on offense. Wrestlers are coached to be aggressive. The general consensus is that it is easier to defeat the opponent by outscoring him than by keeping him from scoring.

One of the severest criticisms of a countering style of wrestling is that it leads to dull and uninteresting contests. Critics suggest that it is too restrictive and defensive. Relying on the opponent to initiate a move, they say, constitutes stalling. Subsequently, penalty points are commonly imposed.

While there may be a certain amount of justification for this accusation, the mode of wrestling presented here is in no way dull or uninteresting. It is, on the contrary, vital and exciting.

The counter control wrestler is aggressively defensive. He reflects an attitude of being aggressively minded and aggressively acting. This is characterized by a mental preparedness for anticipating and, when necessary, initiating appropriate action to avoid or counter any restraining or directing influence attempting to be imposed.

TIMING

Counter control wrestling entails more than waiting for an opponent to initiate an attack. Counters must be timed precisely to take advantage of mistakes. This requires patience and readiness to act.

Opponents will make mistakes. Good opportunities will develop.

Each mistake provides the counter control wrestler with an opportunity to score. He should try to profit from all mistakes. Any one of them could result in his gaining points.

Mistakes are made in two ways. The first is by carelessness or accident. The wrong move is made at the wrong time. The counter control wrestler must not rely solely, however, on the accidental or chance mistakes. Instead, he should devise methods of influencing the opponent into making mistakes.

Inducement is the second way mistakes are made. The counter control wrestler makes them happen. He encourages the opponent to make moves that weaken his position.

Opponents can be expected to take advantage of opportunities to score. Such opportunities can be artificially created as a means of "baiting" an unwary, aggressive opponent.

To bait an opponent is to tempt, entice, or lure him into attempting to capitalize upon what would, from all outward appearances, seem to be a prime opportunity to gain or improve control.

The opponent is thereby unknowingly drawn off guard to an attractive opening for which a counter has been prepared. When he attempts to take advantage of this opportunity, the trap is sprung and the counter applied.

SPECIALIZATION

The countercontrol wrestler must be a specialist. His efforts should be concentrated on mastering a very definite, comparatively limited number of counters. Any counter that does not seem natural should be discarded. It is more beneficial to master a limited number than to have a large repertoire of partially learned ones.

Each wrestler will find it easier to master some counters than others. Rather than trying to perfect a counter that continues to give him trouble, the wrestler should spend time on those which he favors and feel right to him. Those counters which work most successfully for him are the ones he should attempt to perfect. He should master them well enough to be effective against the strongest of foes.

More counters could be learned than ever could be used or needed. The only purpose the coach has for demonstrating a variety of counters is to provide each wrestler with the opportunity to select those best suited to his style. It is important to remember that it is not how many counters the wrestler knows, but how well he can perform the ones he does know.

COUNTERMOVES

In top-notch competition, almost without exception, each attack is followed by a series of countermoves before any points are scored. Consequently, MOST MOVES IN WRESTLING ARE ESSENTIALLY COUNTERMOVES. After each initial attack everything else is counters, and counters to counters. The action continues to be countermoves until one is successful or until the series is terminated and the next offensive tactic is initiated.

DECEPTION

The counter control wrestler must be able to distinguish between a genuine attack and a deceptive move. He must identify feints intended to mislead him into reacting to an imagined danger.

He must not be fooled. Countering a hold that is not forthcoming or one that never truly materializes can be a serious mistake. It may weaken his position and result in actually assisting the opponent in applying the hold.

Good opponents are deceptive. By appearing to do one thing while intent on another they make their goals somewhat easier to attain. A deceptive move to one side, when well executed, can for example, cause a less alert counter control wrestler to commit his weight in a particular direction, thus rendering him vulnerable.

Feints designed to look like the start of some maneuver conceal their actual purpose. They readily fit into the pattern of a real attack.

REACTION

Counter control wrestling is essentially reaction wrestling. To be effective the counter control wrestler must be able to respond instantaneously. Since it is impossible to even begin to counter until the attack has been launched, counters must be employed with remarkable speed.

The counter control wrestler is always at a disadvantage. He never knows WHEN the attack is going to be made, WHERE it will be directed, or WHAT type of attack it will be. In addition, the opponent is generally familar with most, if not all, the defenses commonly used to counter the chosen attack.

DETECTION

The alert counter control wrestler can often sense what the opponent is going to do before he does it. Detection of cues often disclose the direction or type of attack to be attempted.

When advance notice of where the attack is going to be attempted is unknowingly given, the counter control wrestler is able to gain a favorable position to counter. Countering the attack is therefore much easier and obviously much more likely to be successful.

Subtle movements often indicate the direction of the attack. Detecting these movements results in being able to respond more quickly in countering the attack.

It is of vital importance, however, that the counter control wrestler anticipate ACCURATELY. If, for example, he takes one step in the wrong direction, he must then take another step to regain his former position. The time that lapses between taking these two steps may be just long enough for the opponent to complete an attack.

The counter control wrestler must remain alert at all times. It only takes one unthinking split second for the opponent to launch a successful attack.

The counter control man must first avoid being maneuvered out of position by feints; then react instantly by defending himself; and finally, when possible, score by countering.

TEACHING

From a coaching standpoint it is wisest to teach counters in the same manner as any other technique. They should first be demonstrated in their entirity, at the speed and in the manner in which they are expected to be performed after being mastered.

Each counter should then be broken down into its component parts. The movements that make up the counter are then practiced slowly in an attempt to allow the learner to get a feel for the desired pattern and a sense of proper body position.

The partner in this learning situation must be cooperative. He should resist only to the extent necessary for the other wrestler to get the feel of the counter. As the movements become more natural, resistance can gradually be increased. Eventually, the counter should be attempted in situations resembling those encountered in competition. This is best accomplished through scrimmaging and drills.

Countering is largely a matter of reflex. Since a counter cannot be started until the attack has been made, it is important that reflexes be developed. A feeling or sensing of just when and how to employ a counter is essential.

By appraisal and study, counters can be worked out to suit any situation. A portion of every workout should be devoted to "position" or "situation" wrestling. In this type of wrestling, holds are applied before counters are attempted. The pace is slow at first, but gradually increases as the competency of the counter wrestler improves.

Another popular method of practicing counter is in series drills. For example, the roll-reroll-switch-reswitch is a fairly common series. It is conducted in the following manner: first the roll is executed; secondly, the roll-reroll; then, the roll-reroll-switch; and finally, the roll-reroll-switch-reswitch series in its entirety.

4
STRATEGY

TACTICAL SITUATION

In wrestling the attacker always has certain advantages in knowing exactly:

1. WHEN the attack will be tried
2. WHERE the attack will be directed
3. WHAT type of attack will be attempted.

Being the attacker he is able to devote all his energies to exploiting selected weaknesses in the opponent's defense.

The strategy of the counter control wrestler must be to minimize, neutralize, and, when possible, overcome these advantages. He must be constantly aware of all the elements existing in each situation. These include:

1. the score
2. the period
3. the time remaining, and
4. the relative mat position.

OBJECTIVES

The primary objective of the counter control wrestler should be to keep the opponent from scoring. This objective must be uppermost in his mind at all times.

The secondary objective is to score while on the defensive. His offense must be a natural extension or outgrowth of his defense.

These objectives complement each other inasmuch as the fulfillment of one assists in the realization of the other. If prevented from scoring, the opponent is likely to gamble and, thereby, make a greater number of mistakes. This increases the chances of scoring on him.

In order to accomplish his objectives, the counter control wrestler should prepare a defense around those holds most commonly used by the opponent. It should be remembered that wrestlers generally wrestle according to patterns or habits. They have favorite or "pet" holds. These are the holds that have been most successful for them. They are prone to rely on these holds and repeat them frequently. This is particularly true in closely contested matches. It is wisest for the counter control wrestler to plan ahead so as to be prepared for these holds rather than relying on "on-the-spot" strategy.

In planning for a particular opponent it is best to practice those counters which have proven themselves successful against him. This information is readily secured from scouting reports. When pet holds fail the opponent is likely to resort to other holds that he is probably not as efficient at executing.

Interestingly, many of the most common counters are least effective. The rationale is simple. Popular counters are often expected. The attacker is conditioned to anticipate familiar counters.

A relatively uncommon counter is more likely to catch the opponent by surprise. The chances of its success are greater than would be the case if a conventional counter were attempted.

The element of surprise can be a basic key to successful counter control wrestling. If the opponent is unable to readily recognize the counter being employed, he is at a disadvantage.

PSYCHOLOGICAL SETBACK

When the counter control wrestler scores he gains a tremendous psychological advantage. This is due to the fact that the attacker was mentally geared to score. When the opposite occurs he experiences a severe psychological setback. Not only did he fail to score, but in attempting to score he was actually scored on. The shock is often so great that all self-confidence is lost. This manifests itself in the form of an ineffective attack.

5

TAKEDOWN COUNTERS

Counter control wrestling is emphasized to varying degrees by every coach. It can be the great equalizer by compensating for offensive weaknesses. Many wrestlers are excellent competitors sheerly on the basis of their defensive ability. They have developed the necessary skill to turn what would appear on the surface as apparent disasters into triumphant victories.

The counter control wrestler has a good chance of scoring if he can prevent the opponent from wrestling the kind of match he wants to wrestle. By forcing him into a different style he becomes less efficient. For example, if the opponent uses a close tie-up, preventing him from getting in close can be effective. If he prefers a closed stance, wrestling from an open stance can be disconcerting.

A half-hearted or indifferently executed takedown is easily countered. Once the opponent is committed to a takedown, anything less than one hundred percent effort will give the defending wrestler an advantage.

Failing to penetrate is a major reason for the attacker not scoring. By dropping and then having to reach he becomes vulnerable.

The well-coached wrestler is told never to shoot for a takedown without first having set it up. What he is told and what he actually does are not always the same. Failing to initiate some sort of feint or diversionary move prior to shooting provides the counter control wrestler with a distinct advantage.

It is also possible that the attacker will set himself up for a takedown. One of the most common instances of this is immediately following a takedown attempt that is blocked but not countered. There is a natural tendency for him to mentally relax as he begins

24

to back out to resume the neutral position. This slackening of alertness, for just a fraction of a second as the stalemate is being dissolved, makes him vulnerable. A keen counter control wrestler will instinctively sense this and at that precise moment take the initiative to counterattack by shooting in for a takedown.

NEUTRAL POSITION

The teaching of proper stance should begin early in the season. Each coaching point should be described, demonstrated, and reviewed over and over again. The men should be expected to coach themselves and help each other. Their form should continually be checked and corrected.

A sound stance is of utmost importance. The head is up with the eyes primarily focused on the opponent's mid-section. Attention is directed to this area because it is the opponent's least effective faking medium. He may fake with his shoulders, feet, head, or arms, but when his midsection moves, the counter control wrestler can be certain there is no fake involved.

The elbows should be kept close to the sides of the body. When in a tie-up position, the elbow used for tying up should be held perpendicular to the mat in order to defend effectively against leg attacks and go-behinds.

The upper torso should be bent slightly forward at the waist. The back should be kept more vertical than horizontal to the mat.

The feet should be approximately shoulders' width apart with the knees flexed slightly. Most of the body's weight should be over the balls of the feet.

MOVEMENT MECHANICS

Concerning movement, a glide step or shuffle should be employed. This is made on the balls of the feet. By distributing the weight of the body evenly over both legs, mobility is optimal in all directions—forward, rear, and lateral.

The muscles are relaxed. Quick, short, gliding steps are taken. This is not possible if the muscles are tense.

TACTICS

To be successful the counter control wrestler must be:

Neutral position.

1. aggressively defensive
2. position oriented
3. patient and disciplined
4. a specialist.

By being position oriented, the counter control wrestler keeps his back to the mat's edge. This limits the opponent's shooting space and decreases the chances of being taken down inside the boundary lines.

The counter control wrestler should develop safe takedown counters. Failure to do so may result in repeatedly getting into trouble when countering.

Tie-up position.

The counter control wrestler must be careful not to be penalized for stalling. Unfortunately, some officials will force a counter control wrestler to alter his style. In such cases, the official becomes a determining factor in the outcome of the match. Instead of performing his intended function of ensuring that the contest is conducted according to the rules, he mistakenly takes on another role.

Counter #1 to Double-Leg Takedown

Sprawl by extending your legs back and spreading them for balance.

Counter #2 to Double-Leg Takedown

Overhook the opponent's arm while underhooking the other arm as a means of forcing him over to his back.

Drive your legs backward while applying a crossface and reaching for the opponent's ankle.

Keep your legs straight and spread. Do not allow the knees to touch the mat.

Pivot to a position behind the opponent.

Counter #4 to Double-Leg Takedown

Position the arm used for tying up, perpendicular to the mat.

Use the arm as a buffer when opponent drops in for a takedown.

Overhook the opponent's far arm.

Exert force onto his overhooked arm.

Force downward onto the arm while twisting your hips.

Continue applying pressure on the arm and turning your hips.

Place your hand on the opponent's head while starting a cross under step.

Force the opponent to release your legs.

Pivot to a neutral position.

This counter is effective since few opponents expect to have their chins grasped when going for a leg takedown. Reach over the opponent's far arm.

Grasp the opponent's chin while stepping back.

Pull upward on the opponent's chin.

Begin whipping the opponent back in an arclike movement.

Secure a restraining hold.

Counter #7 to Double-Leg Takedown

Apply a quarter nelson as the opponent either goes in for a leg takedown or is backing out.

Use pressure to drive him over.

Swing around to one side as you go into a pinning combination.

Sprawl and apply a crossface as opponent reaches.

Pull in on the crossface while grasping and pulling up on his ankle.

Throw your legs back and release his grip on your leg.

Drive your arm across his face and hook it under his armpit while pivoting toward him on one knee.

Secure a pinning hold after dropping him onto his back.

Sprawl and distribute your weight forward.

Hook an arm around the opponent's knee when he brings it up.

44

Drive him onto his back.

Sprawl and crossface.

Reach through and lock your hands around both of the opponent's arms.

Pull his arms toward you while turning your hips into him.

Work him into a pinning position.

This counter is commonly used as a last resort when the opponent has penetrated deeply. Reach over the opponent's back, grasp both his ankles, and lift.

When your leg picked up, drive it between the opponent's legs. Attempt to keep him from moving in close by pushing on his head and shoulder while placing weight over the captured leg.

Apply a whizzer while placing your instep on the outside of the opponent's thigh. This is the most desirable position for your leg whenever it is captured and lifted.

Employ an arm drag and jerk the opponent forward while reaching around behind his buttocks with the other arm.

Grasp the opponent's hands.

Pull up on his hands while pushing down with your leg.

Continue pushing your leg down while rotating your hips toward him.

Keep your leg high in the opponent's crotch.

Reach out and grasp the opponent's ankle.

Drive into the opponent while pulling up on his ankle.

Sprawl and crossface.

Free your leg while shifting your hand from the crossface position to a position under his armpit.

Use a short arm drag to spin behind.

As your leg is lifted from the mat, turn away from the opponent and vigorously pull your leg free.

Take a firm grip on the opponent's chin and forehead.

Lift his head to the other side of your waist.

Bring your inside leg through while pulling him past you with a rear crotch or a far-ankle hold.

Maintain a stable position by bending forward.

Reach between the opponent's legs in initiating a standing switch.

Drop down to one hip while arching your back.

Come around to a position on top.

Keep your weight over your captured leg while grasping the opponent's wrist.

Insert your hand under his armpit and lift the arm up, keeping it as straight as possible.

Continue lifting the arm until he is forced over onto his back.

Grasp the opponent's wrist while hooking the other hand under his armpit.

Arm drag and swing around to a position behind.

Place weight over the captured leg.

Reach under the opponent's armpit from behind.

Lock your hands.

Pull up on his arm while backing out to a safe position. If necessary apply a whizzer.

Apply a quarter nelson. Straighten your knee and keep your leg well back so the opponent cannot gather it in.

Exert pressure down on his head.

Move to one side as he is turned over onto his back.

Spread your legs while lowering your hips. Keep your legs back and attempt to push away.

To keep the opponent from getting in close, push him away at the shoulder.

Counter #2 to Fireman's Carry

Sprawl as you recognize the fireman's carry being initiated.

Counter #3 to Fireman's Carry

If caught offguard, attempt to attain a cross-body ride by grapevining the opponent's leg and posting your free arm on the mat for balance.

Push hard on the opponent's elbow to remove his hand from your head while working to free your captured leg.

Grasp the opponent's arm above the elbow.

Hook an arm under the opponent's armpit and pry up on it.

Turn the opponent onto his back.

Place a hand on the opponent's elbow.

Shove the elbow away with a full sweeping motion.

Shift your head to a position over the arm being dragged.

As the drag is initiated, drive your body across in front of the opponent's while hooking your heel behind his leg.

Drive into the opponent while pulling back hard with your heel.

As the opponent completes the head drag, hook your arm over his arm.

Jerk down on his arm while throwing your near leg high over his body.

Get perpendicular and apply a pinning combination.

Hook your hand over the opponent's elbow, thereby making it impossible for him to employ the snap down without also being pulled down.

Keep your elbows in, thereby not leaving space for the opponent's head.

As the opponent drops down, bend your knees and crouch, thereby keeping him at a distance.

Cup the opponent's chin as he initiates the duck under.

Back out.

Keep your elbow in and forearm perpendicular to the mat.

As the opponent ducks, bring your arm over the top of his head to wing-lock his arm.

Execute a roll by dropping your shoulder to the mat.

Place a hand behind the opponent's knee.

Lift and fall back.

Pivot and swing around to one side.

Reach around the opponent's neck and cup his chin.

Hop on your free leg just prior to striking it against the rear of the opponent's legs.

Drop back while twisting his chin to one side.

Apply a cradle pin.

Take advantage of the opponent's momentum while being whipped over.

Swing your arm under the opponent's armpit.

Continue around to a position of advantage.

Bend forward while forcing your captured arm away from your body.

Slip your hand between the opponent's arms and grasp his wrist.

Pry up on his forearm.

Turn your wrists down while straightening your arms.

Grasp the opponent's four fingers.

Pull his hand off your wrist.

Straighten your arm.

Turn your wrist up and out.

Shift your weight to your free leg.

Hook your foot behind the opponent's legs while turning toward him.

Drop back and raise the hooked leg.

Arm drag to a position on top.

Be prepared to switch as the opponent trips forward.

As you drop, place an arm back toward the opponent's crotch.

Pivot.

Swing around to a position on top.

Bend forward at the waist as the opponent trips.

Reach down and lock your hands around the opponent's leg.

Gather the opponent's leg in close.

Trip him back to the mat.

Secure a hold of the opponent's arm as he trips.

While the opponent drives forward, post one hand on the mat in front of your opposite foot.

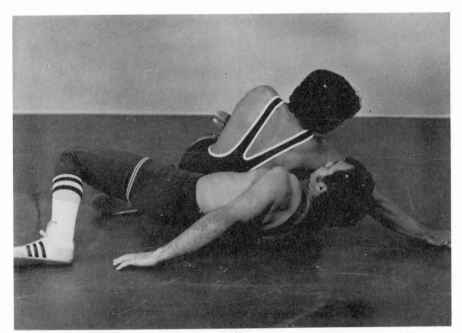

Roll.

Secure control.

Grapevine the opponent's legs as he lifts you.

As he lowers you back to the mat, place a hand against the inside of his thigh while turning.

Drop back and scoot forward.

Go behind for control.

Be prepared to switch as the opponent pulls you back.

Place a hand between his legs.

Turn toward him.

Come to a top position.

Be prepared to switch as the opponent pulls you back.

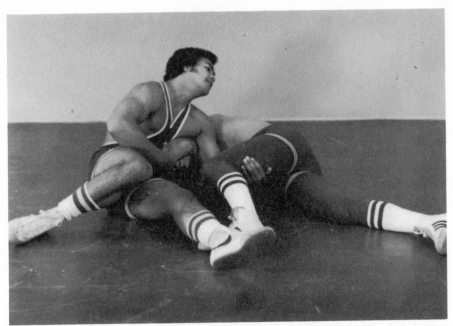

Shift your hips to one side while putting pressure on the opponent's arm.

Complete the move by gaining the position of advantage.

Reach down and grasp the opponent's ankle.

Pull up on the leg.

Apply a cradle pin.

Maintain a stable base.

Bend forward as the opponent steps in front.

Reach down and encircle the opponent's leg.

Lift his leg and drive him to the mat.

6
ESCAPE AND REVERSAL COUNTERS

While on top, the counter control wrestler must be continually aware of the opponent's relative position on the mat. Countering the opponent's efforts to escape and reverse is easiest when he is in a flattened position, becomes harder when he gets to a hands-and-knees position, and most difficult when he stands up. In the standing position, he is very mobile and therefore much harder to counter.

The counter control wrestler is wisest to ride back on the opponent's legs. If the opponent cannot free his legs, he cannot get to a standing position. Therefore, he is limited to attempting escapes from a position down on the mat. Anytime an escape or reversal is tried from down on the mat, the chances are greater of it losing points by being countered than would be the case if attempted from standing. A mistake made on the mat is more likely to result in counter points being scored than a mistake made above the mat.

The counter control wrestler, while on top, should be looking for opportunities to catch the bottom man halfway through a move. By anticipating situations where the opponent is vulnerable, advantage can be taken of his relative position. He must learn to exploit certain positions—back, side, stomach, one or both knees—that the opponent may assume while on the bottom. The most effective counters are, naturally, those which place the opponent on his back.

Opponents who, while on the bottom, take time to think about moves before attempting them will usually attempt these moves much too late and much too slowly to make them successful. A formidable counter control wrestler will generally find it easy to counter any technique that takes time to be thought out before being attempted.

Opponents who permit large segments of time to elapse between initial and subsequent moves are easily beaten. Isolated attempts to escape or reverse can generally be countered with little difficulty.

The difficult opponents are those who execute escape and reversal attempts in series. They link or combine moves so that little time is generally available to prepare for countering each move individually.

REFEREE'S POSITION

Referee's position.

The official rules clearly state the proper position for the wrestler on top. However, some choice in the placement of the head, hands, and feet does exist. The head, for example, although having to be placed over the midline of the opponent's back, may be positioned with some variability in height. Ideally it should be situated so as to permit a clear, unobstructed view of the referee's starting signal.

It is important that the top man allow himself as much maneuverability as possible when assuming the referee's position. He must be prepared to counter the opponent's first move.

MOVEMENT MECHANICS

In this fast-moving sport the top man's greatest asset is mobility. From the referee's position he should be prepared for constant movement while keeping his legs out of the opponent's reach.

The top man is most mobile when he moves on his toes. He can move faster and shift or change directions quicker from this position than from any other. If, however, he allows his knees to touch the mat, he immediately loses mobility. Anytime any part of his uniform touches the mat, mobility decreases.

The top man should plan to keep the opponent in a weakened and off-balanced position. His movement must therefore be carefully planned and not random. He can best counter most escape and reversal attempts by staying behind the opponent.

He should keep the opponent working harder than himself. His weight should be over the opponent in order to wear him down.

He should follow the opponent rather than resist him. To accomplish this he must be relaxed. He can move quickly only if relaxed. When he is tense, energy is wasted and speed hindered.

Opponents will often attempt moves that get them in trouble. Unkowingly they may favor escapes and reversals that place them in positions to be countered.

TACTICS

The counter control wrestler must make things happen. He should encourage the opponent to make mistakes that can readily be capitalized upon.

In the top position he can tempt or entice the bottom man into making mistakes. He can solicit or invite obvious offensive moves. The bottom man can thereby drawn off guard to attempting an anticipated escape or reversal for which a counter has been prepared.

Of all the ways an opponent can be ridden, those which involve gripping a leg are the least risky, safest, and most practical.

Unless the opponent can free his legs he is forced to wrestle from a position down on the mat. Escapes and reversals attempted from down on the mat have a greater chance of losing points by being countered than if attempted from standing. The closer the opponent is to the surface of the mat when he makes a mistake, the greater are the chances of scoring against him.

An opponent is less likely to gain a reversal, two points, and the position of advantage when his legs are controlled. Also, if at anytime difficulty is encountered in riding his legs, they can readily be released. The most the opponent will gain is an escape.

The counter control wrestler should ride in a manner that will keep him out of trouble. He should be able to turn loose of anything he has hold of. He should avoid rides that place him in positions where he is likely to be reversed.

Knowing when to release an opponent is extremely important. The counter control wrestler must recognize when he is having difficulty riding. At this time he must be willing to release the ride rather than risk a reversal and possibly end up on his back. He must not chance the loss of two or more points and the position of advantage. He doesn't have to ride the opponent to beat him.

The top man should not expend any more energy than is necessary to remain in the position of advantage. He should train himself to move as effortlessly as possible. He should remain as relaxed as possible. If he can make the bottom man work harder trying to escape than he has to work to maintain control, the opponent will become fatigued sooner.

The intelligent way to wear the opponent down is to make him carry as much weight as possible. In order to keep as much weight on him as possible, the top man should stay off his knees and move on his toes. This method of moving requires the least amount of effort.

The longer the bottom man has to carry the extra weight of the top man, the sooner he will tire and the slimmer will be his chances of winning. Having to carry a portion of the top man's weight means that the top man's burden is lightened. The opponent thereby unwillingly assists in keeping the top man from fatiguing.

A fatigued opponent is a careless opponent.A careless opponent makes mistakes. Each mistake represents a scoring opportunity for the counter control wrestler. Capitalizing upon these mistakes is basic to counter control wrestling.

The fact that the bottom man has to expend a great deal of

energy carrying his own weight plus part of the top man's, coupled with the fact that the top man has a lightened load, all contributes to the opponent's defeat.

Counter #1 to Whizzer

Grapevine the opponent's leg while placing your arm on his thigh.

Step over the opponent's near leg and grasp his knee from the inside.

Lift his leg high, thereby forcing him onto his back.

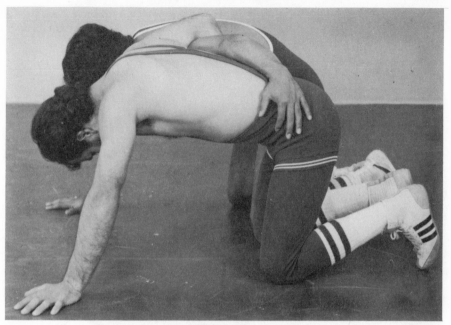

Keep your head up and knees well spread.

Straighten your arm out to the rear, keeping the palm up.

Swing the arm forward forcefully.

Move the arm back to a position of control.

Counter #4 to Whizzer

Resist the opponent's efforts to drive you to the mat.

Duck your head and reach through the opponent's crotch.

137

Roll completely under.

Follow through to a position of advantage.

Move out to one side and apply a half nelson.

Lock your hands under the opponent's armpit.

Power him to his back.

Keep your head higher than your opponent's.

Reach for the opponent's far arm.

Catch his arm as he pulls it back.

Clamp on a half nelson.

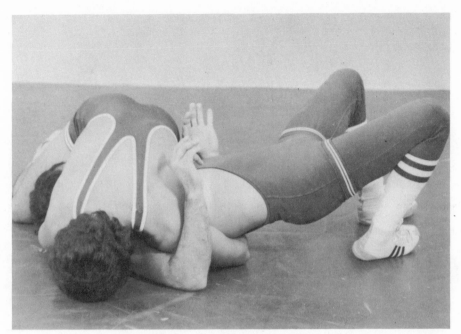

Secure the half-nelson pin.

Hook the opponent's near leg.

Push on his head while moving your arm down to the thigh of his hooked leg.

Encircle his leg, thereby breaking the whizzer hold and gaining control.

Keep your knees well spread for balance.

Bring your hand over the opponent's shoulder.

Lock your hands.

Pry the opponent's arm forward.

147

Go to a pinning combination.

Step forward with the outside leg.

Interlock your arms around him as he straightens up.

Whip him over backward in a clockwise direction.

Secure a position of advantage.

Keep your head higher than your opponent's.

Sit through, bringing the opponent's leg with you.

Place a hand under his knee.

Force him onto his back.

152

Place your head against the opponent's stomach and secure a hold on his far leg as he reaches to switch.

Grip under the opponent's shoulders.

Shift one hand to his chin.

Move to one side while turning his chin to the mat.

Place one hand under the opponent's knee.

Tilt him back to one side.

Move to one side while placing one arm around the opponent's neck and the other behind his knee.

Lock your hands, drop him back to the mat, and overhook his free leg.

Press forward on the opponent's upper back.

Quickly spin to the front.

Force him over into a pinning situation.

Maintain a secure grip on the opponent's shoulders.

As the opponent turns, begin dragging him past you.

Complete the drag by securing a rear crotch hold.

Maintain a grip on the opponent's braced arm.

Destroy his position by pulling the braced arm back and driving him onto his side.

162

Raise your near leg up.

Limp arm by bringing your hand forward with the palm up.

Whip the arm back and pick up one of the opponent's legs.

Force the opponent onto his back.

Keep your head up.

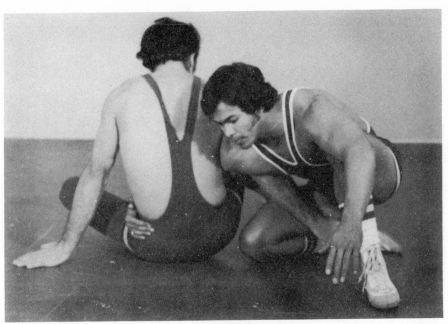

Lift your knee off the mat.

Sit through.

Secure a rear crotch hold to assist you in turning.

Shift your weight to your far leg.

Lock your arm around the opponent's switching arm.

Throw your leg across the opponent's body.

Step across with both legs and secure a perpendicular position.

Counter #1 to Outside Roll

Thrust your legs back and keep your hips low as the opponent starts to roll.

Counter #2 to Outside Roll

Jump across to the far side as the opponent starts to roll.

Obtain a rear crotch hold as the opponent starts to roll.

Lift on his thigh and begin to roll through.

Using his momentum, come to a position on top.

Post your leg while attempting to free your anchored arm.

Shift your weight to your outside leg.

Hook your inside leg around the opponent's inside leg.

Thrust an arm through and behind the opponent's leg.

Drive him back to the mat.

Crowd the opponent by stepping in front and overhooking his leg.

Trip him to the mat by pulling back on the leg while driving forward.

Pick up the opponent's ankle while sweeping his supporting leg back.

Maintain control as he drops to the mat.

Place a foot behind the opponent's heel.

Forcefully pull him back while turning and dropping to one side.

Grasp the opponent's ankles while placing your shoulder against his thighs.

Pull back on the ankles while driving him forward to the mat.

Hoist the opponent up while sweeping his legs.

Bring him back to the mat under control.

Hook an arm behind the opponent's thigh.

184

Lift the leg off the mat.

Pivot to bring him back to the mat.

Secure an inside crotch ride.

Place one arm over the opponent's neck and the other between his legs.

Connect your hands and roll him into a cradle pin.

Step across behind the opponent.

Trip him back to the mat under control.

7

RIDE COUNTERS

Most rides involve controlling either the bottom man's arms or legs, or a combination thereof. If the bottom man can keep his arms and legs free from being controlled the following rides cannot be applied:

Near arm and near leg
Near arm and far leg
Far arm and near leg
Far arm and far leg
Crossbody
Head lever
Waist and near leg
Waist and far leg
Waist and near arm
Waist and far arm.

While he is down on the mat the bottom man's weight should rest mainly over his knees. This makes it possible for him to move his hands quickly. By keeping his hands free and mobile he is able to counter the opponent's efforts to control them. His lower torso is also less easily controlled in this position.

In order to counter ankle rides he must either hide his ankle, move it out of the opponent's reach, or, if already captured, place weight over it while reaching back to free it.

The counter control wrestler's offense should be a natural outgrowth of his defense. This is well expressed by Kenney and Law in the following passage:

Many wrestlers are taught to assume a purely defensive position. They believe they have a better opportunity of escaping and reversing if they let their opponent make the first movement from the top position. This type of wrestling is commonly called "counterwrestling" and is very effective. It is based on the theory of forcing the top man to take undue chances in trying to break down the under man, who then capitalizes on the openings created.*

To score, the bottom man must counter the top man's control. A two-point reversal and the position of advantage is, of course, preferable to a one-point escape.

Oftentimes, an opponent will mistakenly favor rides that place him in positions where he is likely to be countered. For example, riding with an arm around the bottom man's waist can get him into trouble. By anchoring this arm, the bottom man often sets up a counter to the ride being employed.

There are at least three common reversals that can effectively be employed against an opponent who rides in this manner. If pulling, the top man can be switched. If pushing, he can be rolled. If neither pulling or pushing, he can be whizzered.

REFEREE'S POSITION

There are varied starting positions that can be assumed. All have certain advantages and disadvantages. The two distinct advantages of the starting position suggested here are, first, while in this position it is very difficult for the opponent to apply an effective ride; and second, the bottom man is in the best position to counter most attacking moves.

Hands—The hands should be kept approximately shoulder's width apart with the fingers cupped and the arms slightly bent at the elbows. The palms should be kept as close to the knees as the rules will permit and turned in slightly. Maximal stability and a coillike potential in rising from the mat are hereby realized.

Head—The head should be kept high. If the head is lowered, the wrestler is at a kinesiologic disadvantage and susceptible to cradles and nelsons.

Harold E. Kenney and Glenn C. Law. *Wrestling*. New York: McGraw-Hill Book Co., Inc., 1952, p. 79.

Referee's position.

Body Weight—The body's weight should be distributed back and over the knees and legs as opposed to being over the hands and arms. The center of gravity is kept low by shifting the weight of the body to a position over the haunches. This complements efforts to keep from having the head driven to the mat if one of the supporting limbs is removed by the opponent.

Knees—The knees should be slightly more than hips' width apart. This provides a sound base that will not easily be destroyed.

Toes—The toes should be dug into the mat and turned under. This facilitates a forward and upward springlike action in rising from the mat.

MOVEMENT MECHANICS

The counter control wrestler should, as often as possible, attempt to counter rides after gaining a standing posture. Although a large number of popular counters can be employed from down on the mat, none is preferable to those from standing. Any counter to a ride executed from down on the mat has an equal if not greater chance of losing points than one performed from standing. Points are most commonly lost when a counter is successful within inches of the surface of the mat.

TACTICS

The crux of the bottom man's efforts to counter the top man's control should be focused upon exploiting the opponent's movements and riding positions. For example, when the opponent is working for a breakdown, the counter control wrestler should exploit his efforts by moving a bit further than he anticipates. The combined resulting forces thereby can be effectively employed to counter the opponent's control.

Also, by being position oriented it is possible for the bottom man to use the edge of the mat, discriminately, of course, as a means of regaining the referee's position in the middle of the mat. This is particularly desirable in the event that difficulty is encountered in countering cross-body rides.

Counter #1 to Hand Control

Bring your open hand vigorously across the front of your body.

Strike the opponent's fingers with the heel of your hand.

Counter #2 to Hand Control

Raise your hand up while flexing the elbow.

Straighten the arm momentarily.

Rotate the arm outward and forward.

Keep the back straight while reaching for the fingers of the opponent's hand.

Pry up on his fingers while rotating the other hand in a circular movement against his thumb.

Rotate both arms downward and outward.

Straighten the arms out to the sides.

Place weight on your hand.

Bend the elbow while sliding it forward.

Get the opponent's weight off your back.

Reach under the opponent's leg and lift it.

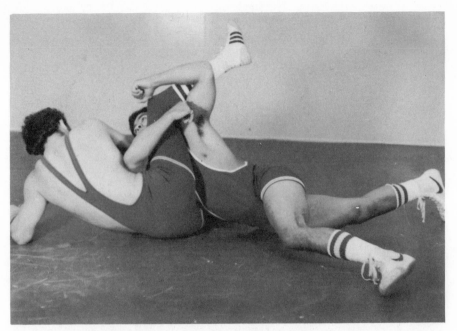

Scoot down while turning into the opponent.

Work into a position of control.

Counter #2 to Cross Body

Catch the opponent's leg as he attempts to insert it.

Counter #3 to Cross Body

Straighten your leg as the opponent attempts to apply the ride.

Counter #4 to Cross Body

Bring your legs tightly together to prevent the opponent from obtaining the ride.

Counter #5 to Cross Body

Straighten your grapevined leg.

Pull down on the opponent's arm.

Slide your arm between his body and your's.

Come to a position of control on top.

Whip your arm around the opponent's back.

Pull down with force.

Step over to a position of control.

Secure a hold on the opponent's arm.

Grasp the opponent's leg just below the knee and straighten your grape-vined leg.

Turn and scissor your legs.

Grasp the opponent's hand.

Extend the leg.

Bring the leg forward.

Underhook the opponent's arm while simultaneously extending your leg.

Place your foot against the opponent's wrist.

Shove back on his wrist, thereby forcing him to release the ankle.

Work to maintain a stable base.

212

Raise up while grasping the opponent's arm.

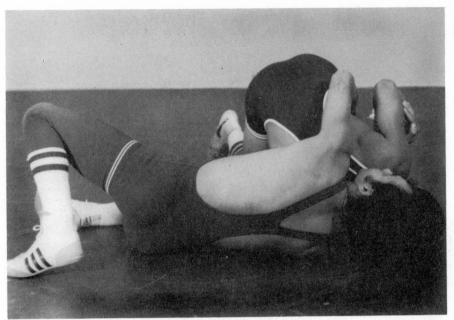

Snap the opponent's arm down to the mat.

Step over the opponent to a position on top.

When the opponent reaches across, apply an overarm hook.

Pull the arm in tight.

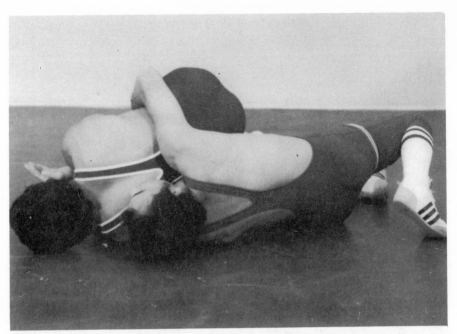

Snap your shoulder down to the mat.

Step over to the far side to gain control.

Come to a sitting posture.

Push down on the opponent's head.

Slide your near leg back and scissor to a neutral position.

Turn to one side.

Keep the opponent's hands busy.

Execute a high bridge.

Turn quickly when he loosens the hold.

Roll to the side the scissors is hooked.

Work an arm under the opponent's leg.

Lie back and lift on the leg.

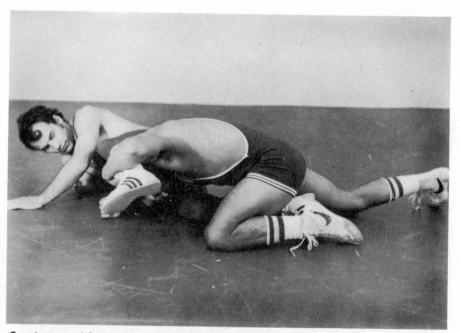

Continue to lift, pulling the leg overhead while turning toward the opponent's head.

Lock your hands over the opponent's knee while straightening your hooked leg.

Turn toward the opponent when the hook is broken.

222

Plant your hands wide on the mat while thrusting your buttocks high.

Start to shake the opponent off with an up-and-down motion.

Continue to shake rapidly as the opponent slips over your head.

Back out between his legs and assume a riding position.

8
PIN COUNTERS

The best time to counter a pinning hold is before it is applied. It is simpler to counter attempts to apply a pinning hold than it is to counter a pinning hold after it has been applied. It is much easier to prevent it from being secured than it is to get free once it is secured.

Fighting out of a pinning hold can be very fatiguing. Having to battle in order to break it results in never quite having the same pep during the remainder of the match.

In countering pins, the bottom man should be alert to two things. First, many opponents are effective with only one pinning combination. If unable to use their hold, they often become careless, make mistakes, and thereby become vulnerable. Second, it takes a considerable amount of ingenuity to pin a wrestler skilled at avoiding pinning situations. Well-trained opponents are generally not content with winning by decisions. They go for the pins. In an effort to turn the bottom men over they may often become overzealous. Being overzealous makes them careless, and carelessness makes them vulnerable.

PINNING POSITION

The most popular and commonly employed pinning hold is the half nelson. Some basic rules for avoiding a half nelson are:

Head—Keep your head up and turned away from the opponent (look away).

Hands—Keep your arms in close to the sides of the body. Do not leave space for the opponent to apply a half nelson. Prevent the opponent from securing leverage by removing his hand from the back of your head or neck.

Body Weight—Move your body parallel to the opponent's (as opposed to perpendicular).

Legs—Keep your far leg out to one side as a brace to prevent the opponent from driving you over onto your back.

MOVEMENT MECHANICS

Pinning situations commonly occur following a takedown or reversal. To avoid the application of a pinning hold, the counter control wrestler should immediately turn onto his stomach whenever taken down or reversed. From a flattened position he should work to regain the hands-and-knees position, and eventually get to standing.

TACTICS

Come up off the mat as often as possible. Standing is the safest position. Since points are awarded in accordance with the proximity of the shoulders to the mat surface, it is wisest to gain altitude quickly and work to maintain it.

The further the shoulders are kept from the mat, the harder it is to be controlled. The harder it is to be controlled, the more difficult it is for the opponent to score.

Turn your head away and look up. Move your leg out to the side as a brace. Reach up, while keeping your elbow in, and pull the opponent's hand off your neck.

Keep your feet spread while pushing on the opponent's thigh.

Bridge high.

At the highest point in the bridge drop suddenly and drive an arm between your chest and the opponent's.

Turn onto your stomach by scissoring your legs.

Push against the opponent's leg to encourage him to bring it forward.

When he brings the leg forward, hook an arm under it.

232

Lock your hands.

Start to roll by pulling in on the opponent's legs and bridging.

Turn and come on top.

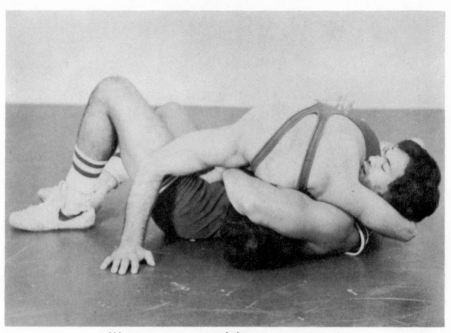

Wrap an arm around the opponent's neck.

Begin turning.

Continue to turn while moving to the far side.

Come to a position on top.

Bring your inside arm off the mat.

Reach up and grasp the opponent's fingers.

Peel the opponent's hand away while looking away.

Counter #2 to Half Nelson from Knees

Lift your head up.

Bring your outside leg forward.

Straighten your back and raise up.

Turn in toward the opponent by pivoting on your knee.

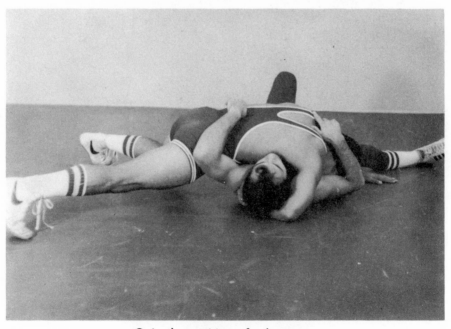

Gain the position of advantage.

Overhook the opponent's arm.

Snap your shoulder down to the mat.

Swing your legs across his body.

Secure a pinning combination.

Grasp the opponent's arm just above the elbow.

Raise your inside knee off the mat.

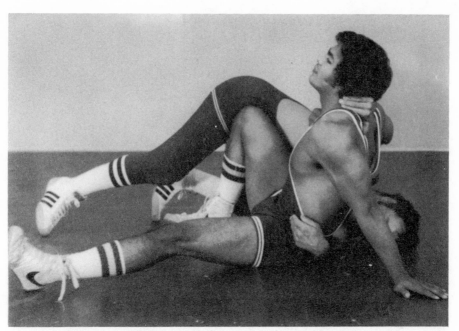

Sit through while pulling down on the opponent's arm.

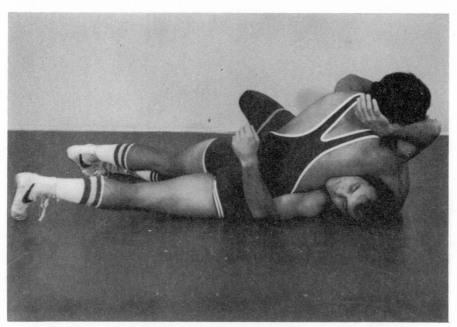

Keep pulling down on the arm while turning to a position on top.

Begin moving your hooked arm forward.

Continue sliding your hooked arm forward while dropping to one side.

Look up while pressing your upper back against the opponent's shoulder.

Drive your elbow between bodies while turning in toward the opponent.

Come to a controlling position.

Counter #1 to Arm Lock

Bring your leg up as near to a right angle as possible.

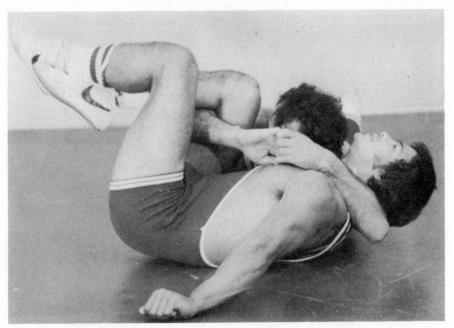

Overhook your cradled leg with your free leg.

Extend your legs while driving your head back.

Bull your neck.

Flatten out while raising your head and looking away.

Bridge up while placing your inside arm close to your chest.

Drop to the mat, shoot your arm through, and turn away.

Continue turning away.

Work to regain an all-fours position.

Counter #1 to Three-Quarter Nelson

Bull your neck.

Look away while sliding your near arm forward along the mat.

Flatten out so your head cannot be turned under.

GLOSSARY

BAIT. To tempt, entice, or lure an opponent into weakening his position by presenting him with an attractive opening for which a counter has been prepared.

BLOCK. To stop or prevent the application of a hold. It does not, as compared to a counter, have the potential for scoring.

CONTROL. To exercise a restraining or directing influence over an opponent.

COUNTER. A maneuver in opposition to an attack that has the potential for developing into an offensive maneuver.

FEINT. A preliminary move initiated with the purpose of enhancing the chances of making a secondary move successful.

TELEGRAPH. To unknowingly give advance notice of a move prior to attempting it, thereby resulting in it being less likely to succeed and more easily countered.

BIBLIOGRAPHY

Buzzard, Don, and Marcucci, Vic. "Takedown Counters—." *The Predicament* (November 15, 1974), p. 10.

Camaione, David N. "Use of Hands in Defensive Position." *Scholastic Coach* (September 1968), pp. 50ff.

Carson, Ray F. *Championship Wrestling—An Anthology*. San Diego, California: Ray Carson, P.O. Box 8171, 1974.

Carson, Ray F. *Championship Wrestling: Coaching to Win*. South Brunswick, New Jersey: A. S. Barnes and Co., Inc., 1974.

———. "Criteria for the Selection of Escapes and Reversals." *Scholastic Coach* (January 1970), pp. 69-70.

———. *The Encyclopedia of Championship Wrestling Drills*. South Brunswick, New Jersey: A. S. Barnes and Co., Inc., 1974.

———. "Standing Vs. On the Mat Escapes and Reversals." *Scholastic Coach* (May 1970), pp. 16-18.

———. *Systematic Championship Wrestling*. South Brunswick, New Jersey: A. S. Barnes and Co., Inc., 1973.

——— and Buel R. Patterson. *Principles of Championship Wrestling*. South Brunswick, New Jersey: A. S. Barnes and Co., Inc., 1972.

Creek, Frank. "Conventional and Unconventional." *Athletic Journal* (October 1971), pp. 40ff.

———. "Counters to the Nelson Family." *Athletic Journal* (June 1971), pp. 48-51ff.

Fornicola, Larry. "Countering the Whizzer." *Scholastic Coach* (October 1968), pp. 38ff.

Frazier, Alexander S. "Countering the Stand Up." *Scholastic Coach* (February 1973), pp. 14-15ff.

Gardner, Sprig. "Basic Checks." *Scholastic Coach* (March 1951), pp. 18-20.

Johnson, Cal. "Single Leg Counter . . . The Raider." *Scholastic Wrestling News* (October 22, 1973), pp. 8-9.

Jones, Gomer, and Wilkinson, Charles (Bud). *Modern Defensive Football*. Englewood Cliffs, New Jersey: Prentice-Hall, Inc., 1960.

Karpal, Frank. "Counters Used in Stand Up Wrestling." *Athletic Journal* (January 1963), pp. 14-16ff.

———. "Offensive Counter Stand Up." *Athletic Journal* (February 1963), pp. 20ff.

Kenney, Harold E., and Law, Glenn C. *Wrestling.* New York: McGraw-Hill Book Co., Inc., 1952.

Kraft, Kenneth. "Takedown Counters and Counterattacks." *Athletic Journal* (November 1966), pp. 46ff.

Leyshon, Glynn A. "Attack Philosophy in Wrestling." *Scholastic Coach* (January 1971), p. 69.

Martin, George. *The Mechanics of Wrestling.* Madison, Wisconsin: College Printing & Typing Co., Inc., 1961.

Rettke, Gary. "Strategy from the Defensive Starting Position." *Scholastic Coach* (December 1972), pp. 32-33.

Riccio, Dennis. "Outside Switch Counters." *Scholastic Coach* (November 1970), pp. 12-13.

————. "Whizzer Counters." *Athletic Journal* (January 1971), pp. 64-65ff.

Sacchi, John. "A Strong Set of Stand Up Counters." *Scholastic Coach* September 1973), pp. 106-7.

Sowers, Chuck. "Countering the Half Nelson." *Scholastic Wrestling News* (November 15, 1972), pp. 14-15.

Swan, Banks. "Turning Defense into Offense." *The Predicament* (January 11, 1973), pp.8ff.

Tillman, Ken. "The Series to Control and Pin." *Athletic Journal* (December 1969), pp. 52-57ff.

Weiss, Steven A. "Controlling the Hands and Wrists." *Athletic Journal* (November 1972), pp. 24-25ff.

————. "Controlling the Head in Wrestling." *Athletic Journal* (December 1967), pp. 16-17ff.

————. "Counters for Single and Double Leg Takedowns." *Scholastic Coach* (September 1968), pp. 30-31.

INDEX